MW00633629

THE FORTH BRIDGE

Botanic GARDENS

EDINBURGH WHISKY

Leith

QUEEN STREET

The Scott MONUMENT

LEITH WALK

Calton HILL

The Forth BRIDGE

PRINCES STREET

STATION

NORTH BRIDGE

Scottish National GALLERY

THE ROYAL MILE

SOUTH BRIDGE

Holyrood PALACE

Edinburgh CASTLE

GRASSMARKET

Greyfriars KIRKYARD

National Museum of SCOTLAND

CLERK STREET

PLEASANCE

QUEENS DRIVE

Scottish PARLIAMENT Building

Holyrood PARK

Arthur's SEAT

University of EDINBURGH

The Meadows

Edinburgh
MAP

N
W E
S

THE
EDINBURGH
ART BOOK

Published by UIT Cambridge Ltd

www.uit.co.uk

PO Box 145, Cambridge CB4 1GQ, England

Phone: +44 (0) 1223 302 041

First published in 2019, in England.

Reprinted in 2020.

ISBN: 978-1-906860-92-9 (hardback)

ISBN: 978-1-906860-93-6 (ePub)

ISBN: 978-1-906860-94-3 (pdf)

Also available for Kindle.

3 5 7 9 10 8 6 4 2

THE
EDINBURGH
ART BOOK

THE CITY THROUGH THE EYES OF ITS ARTISTS

EDITED BY

EMMA BENNETT

UIT
CAMBRIDGE

Acknowledgements

The Edinburgh Art Book has been made possible by the enthusiasm of the contributing artists and to them I am eternally grateful, you are an inspirational bunch.

To the background sound of bagpipes, an illustrious panel of local art and city experts helped select the images for publication and I am indebted to them for their creative input. They are:

- Peter Bourhill (*Editor: Edinburgh Life Magazine*)

- Helen Brown (*Director: ArtSquat*)

- Jonathan Gibbs (*Head of Illustration: Edinburgh College of Art*)

- Ruth MacGilp (*Gallery Manager, Coburg House*)

- Zakia Moulaoui (*Founder: Invisible Cities*)

- David Patterson (*Curatorial and Conservation Manager: Museums and Galleries, Edinburgh*)

I thank Sheila Stickley and Niall Mansfield at UIT / Green Books for their enthusiasm and continued support for *The City Art Book* Series.

To my husband Craig Bennett, thank you for always offering encouragement (and curry or coffee when needed). To Molly and William, I am so proud of you both. Thanks to my Mom, Toni, Great Aunty Jean, Len and Val and all the Bennett/Birch family.

Thanks to all my lovely friends for general book ramblings and support (special nod to Lynn Fraser, Emma Ayling and to Sarah Ramsey for help early on). Thank you to Sarah Maddocks for always listening. Thanks to chief proof reader Alison Schuldt, David Patterson and The City Arts Centre and Peter Bourhill for his knowledge of all things Edinburgh. 'Cheers' to Helen Brown for letting me share your 'Stair' for a night, the speedy tour of Edinburgh and for the Leith gig.

CONTENTS

FOREWORD

This is the city I have lived and worked in all my life. Edinburgh is a place of many moods, of northern skies, of jagged stone and warm hearths. It is a city where old meets new, where tangled medieval buildings neighbour neoclassical splendour. It is the home of the eighteenth century's Enlightenment but also present day inequalities. Here history and fiction walk side by side. Geographically it is a city sculpted by both fire and ice, with topography that rises and falls like an angry sea. From the vantage points of Castle Rock or Arthur's Seat, the terrain plunges down to the valleys of Dean or Colinton, the fluctuations in height providing sudden and dramatic views peeped through archways and closes, or grandly framed by wide Georgian streets. Turning north, one looks toward Fife and the Lomond Hills; east where on a clear day the Bass Rock shines white against deep blue; or south towards the Pentlands Hills, glowing eerily through a winter haar. It is a city that has inspired writers, poets and artists for centuries, no more so than today.

I am delighted to introduce *The Edinburgh Art Book*, celebrating the best city in the world. In this volume and accompanying map, we are taken on a journey through Edinburgh, following in the footsteps of her artists and seeing the multifaceted capital through their eyes. Through the work of the 67 contributing artists we are invited to revel in the beauty of Edinburgh, to view familiar scenes afresh, but more importantly explore the city from unique, undiscovered perspectives.

Here we celebrate Edinburgh's dynamism, her intrigue and her vibrant spirit. Congratulations to the selection panel and the artists: this carefully curated selection of work has led even a seasoned native like me to see Edinburgh anew. And to Edinburgh herself – Lang may yer lum reek!

Tommy Zyw
Director, The Scottish Gallery, Edinburgh

PREFACE

If you stand at the top of Castle Hill in Edinburgh and look out, what you will see is a well-constructed picture. The North Sea provides a background of blue, whilst the foreground is made up of a mosaic of slate rooftops, old tenement buildings and industrial warehouses mixed with transport hubs, green spaces and contemporary architecture. Throw in a castle and streets alive with music and non-stop festivals and you have the unique masterpiece that is Edinburgh.

The Edinburgh Art Book shows the city through the eyes of 67 artists it inspires. Familiar scenes and iconic buildings are interpreted in different ways using a range of media and styles. Look at the city through the eyes of its artists – look at the details they have seen – and you are sure to discover something new.

Local Edinburgh folk will see fresh interpretations of the familiar in the pages of this book, whilst visitors and tourists will be inspired to climb Edinburgh's famous steps or walk the cobbled streets to stand in the footsteps of an artist. It's all here to see – from the vibrant streets you'll find on a walk out to Leith over to the amazing bridges that span the Firth of Forth.

The Edinburgh Art Book is the third in the City Art Book Series (which includes *The Cambridge Art Book* and *The Oxford Art Book*) and represents just some of the talented artists working in Edinburgh and around. Have a look at the credits section in the back to find out about the artists and their work. Hopefully you will find yourself inspired to explore further both the artists and their city.

Emma Bennett
Editor

EDINBURGH CASTLE, SUE SCULLARD
PREVIOUS TWO PAGES: OLD TOWN, VIEW FROM SCOTT MONUMENT, MARIA DOYLE

EDINBURGH CASTLE, KATE MILLER

11

EDINBURGH CASTLE FROM CALTON HILL, ROB HAIN

EDINBURGH CASTLE, PAM MCKENZIE

12

EDINBURGH FROM THE EAST, ALASDAIR BANKS

EDINBURGH CASTLE, JANE ASKEY

EDINBURGH CASTLE, BOB LEES

EDINBURGH CASTLE DARKNESS, ROSS MACINTYRE

TOWARDS EDINBURGH CASTLE, RICHARD BRIGGS

EDINBURGH CASTLE, LIBBY WALKER

EDINBURGH CASTLE VIEW, ANNIE MAY ADAM
FOLLOWING TWO PAGES: EDINBURGH CASTLE, JONATHAN CHAPMAN

17

ROYAL ACADEMY AND EDINBURGH CASTLE, JOHN STOA

THE VENNEL, LAURA CAROLAN

USHER HALL, LOTHIAN ROAD, ROB HAIN

EDINBURGH CASTLE (WINTER), JANE ASKEY

EDINBURGH CASTLE, FRANCIS BOAG

EDINBURGH CASTLE FIREWORKS, LYNN HANLEY

THE MOUND, KATE MILLER

THE GRASSMARKET, COLM O'BRIEN

EDINBURGH CASTLE, JOHN STOA

THE VENNEL, ALAN GLASGOW

EDINBURGH FIREWORKS, ALASDAIR BANKS

FIREWORKS AT EDINBURGH CASTLE, COLM O'BRIEN

EDINBURGH FESTIVAL, CLAIRE HEMINSLEY

EDINBURGH FRINGE FESTIVAL ON THE ROYAL MILE, SALLY J FISHER

MARCHMONT LINKS, LYNN HANLEY

OVER THE TOP OF EDINBURGH, EMMA BENNETT

RAMSAY GARDEN, ADRIAN B McMURCHIE

RAMSAY GARDEN, MOY MACKAY

31

OBSCURA VIEW, SUSIE WRIGHT

THE HUB ON THE ROYAL MILE, COLM O'BRIEN

GLADSTONE'S LAND, FIONA MILLER

TAKE ME UP THE ROYAL MILE, ADRIAN B McMURCHIE

THE WRITERS' MUSEUM, SAM BLAIR

THE WRITERS' MUSEUM, YVETTE EARL

St Giles' Cathedral, Richard Briggs

EDINBURGH OLD TOWN, KAREN WARNER

ADVOCATE'S CLOSE, SOPHIE MARTIN

CANONGATE TOLBOOTH, THE ROYAL MILE, MARIA DOYLE

JOHN KNOX'S HOUSE, ESTHER SEMMENS

CANONGATE KIRK, MOY MACKAY

CANONGATE KIRK, ADRIAN B McMURCHIE

THE SCOTTISH PARLIAMENT, LIANA MORAN

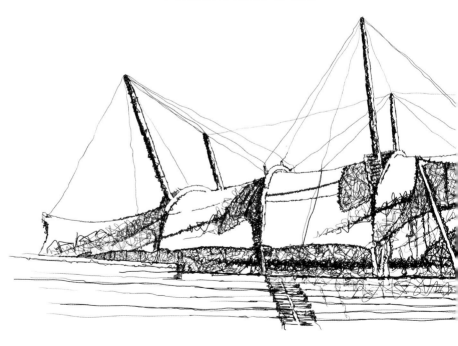

THE SCOTTISH PARLIAMENT (FROM REGENT'S ROAD), CAT OUTRAM

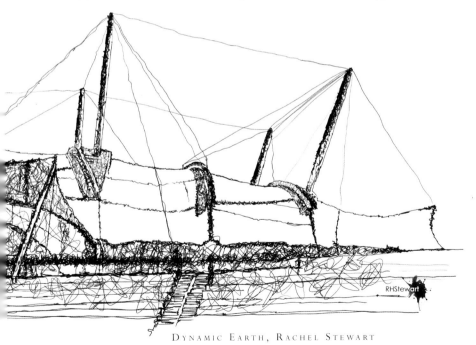

DYNAMIC EARTH, RACHEL STEWART

PALACE OF HOLYROODHOUSE, RICHARD BRIGGS

ARTHUR'S SEAT, SOPHIE MARTIN

ARTHUR'S SEAT, EMILY INGREY-COUNTER

SALISBURY CRAGS, SOPHIE MARTIN

THE MOUND, HILKE MACINTYRE

PRINCES STREET WITH SCOTT MONUMENT AND CALTON HILL, JOHN STOA

SCOTT MONUMENT

EDINBURGH

The Scott Monument, Dave Thompson

THE SCOTT MONUMENT, FIONA MILLER

THE SCOTT MONUMENT, AMANDA PHILLIPS THE SCOTT MONUMENT, LIANA MORAN

52

THE SCOTT MONUMENT, LIAM DOBSON

EDINBURGH PIPER AND THE SCOTT MONUMENT, SALLY J FISHER

NATIONAL GALLERY, VICTORIA ROSE BALL

ST JOHN'S CHURCH IN EDINBURGH'S WEST END, COLM O'BRIEN

CASTLE FROM PRINCES ST, BOB LEES

BALMORAL TOWER, DIANA SAVOVA

JENNERS, EILIDH MULDOON

THE SCOTSMAN STEPS, LINDSEY LAVENDER

STROLL ON VICTORIA STREET, ADRIAN B MCMURCHIE

VICTORIA STREET, SUSIE WRIGHT

WEST BOW 2018, ANDREW SIDDALL

THE COWGATE, TOMASZ MIKUTEL

THE GRASSMARKET, BLYTHE SCOTT

VICTORIA STREET, SAM BLAIR

GREYFRIARS, ANNIE MAY ADAM

MERCHANT STREET, LUCY ROSCOE

NATIONAL MUSEUM OF SCOTLAND, VICTORIA ROSE BALL

BRISTO SQUARE, LIBBY WALKER

OLD COLLEGE, UNIVERSITY OF EDINBURGH, MARIA DOYLE

OLD TOWN, SHEENAGH HARRISON

Arthur's Seat and Edinburgh Old Town, Jane Askey

EDINBURGH CITYSCAPE, JENNI DOUGLAS
RIGHT: EDINBURGH, IAN SCOTT MASSIE

EDINBURGH SKYLINE AT NIGHT, HANNAH KELLY

COLONY HOUSE, PAUL ISAACS

OLD TOWN, KATE MILLER

OLD TOWN, ANNA MIDDLEMASS

VIEW FROM THE OUTLOOK TOWER, SUE SCULLARD

EDINBURGH, PAMELA SCOTT

EDINBURGH SKYLINE, PAMELA SCOTT

OLD TOWN EDINBURGH, ANDREW HAMILTON

EDINBURGH (AFTER PIRANESI), ALASDAIR BANKS

EDINBURGH

VIEW OF OLD COLLEGE, VICTORIA ROSE BALL

81

RAINY SKYLINE, CASSANDRA HARRISON

A N E D I N B U R G H D A Y , J E N N I D O U G L A S

CALTON HILL, BLYTHE SCOTT

VIEW FROM CALTON HILL, ESTHER SEMMENS

CALTON HILL, EILIDH MULDOON
FOLLOWING TWO PAGES: VIEW TO CALTON HILL, ESTHER SEMMENS

Hemmens

DEACON BRODIES, MOY MACKAY

VICTORIA STREET, BLYTHE SCOTT

CAFE ROYAL, ROSS MACINTYRE

LA MAISON BLEUE, BLYTHE SCOTT

GREAT STUART STREET, LUCY JONES

AINSLIE PLACE, LUCY JONES

BOTANIC GARDENS, VICTORIA ROSE BALL

ANN STREET, LAURA GRESSANI

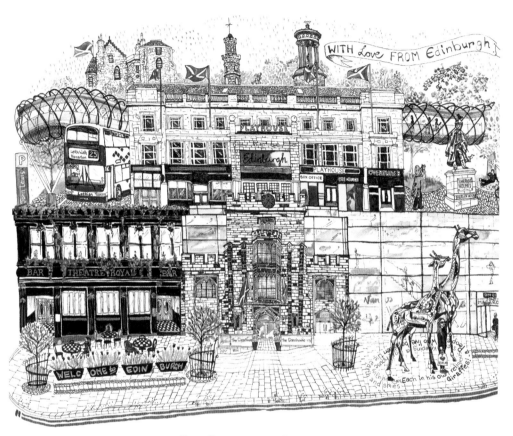

THE PLAYHOUSE, LIBBY WALKER

THE AUDITORIUM INSIDE THE LYCEUM THEATRE, GRINDLAY STREET,
LYDIA BOURHILL

MARCHMONT, SOPHIE MARTIN

SLEDGING, WARRANDER PARK, ROSS MACINTYRE

TOLLCROSS, TENEMENT BACK GREEN, ROB HAIN

FORTH RAIL BRIDGE, IAN SCOTT MASSIE

THE BRIDGES OF THE FORTH FROM SOUTH QUEENSFERRY, ROB HAIN

FORTH RAIL BRIDGE, CLAIRE HEMINSLEY

FORTH RAIL BRIDGE, LUCY JONES

FORTH RAIL BRIDGE, RICHARD BRIGGS

FORTH RAIL BRIDGE, ESTHER SEMMENS

FORTH RAIL BRIDGE, SOPHIE MARTIN

edinburgh

THREE BRIDGES, SCOTT NAISMITH

FORTH RAIL BRIDGE, DAVID HARDCASTLE

101

THE THREE FORTH BRIDGES, COLM O'BRIEN

THE THREE BRIDGES, LIAM DOBSON

DEAN VILLAGE, REBECCA HESELTON

DEAN VILLAGE, KATE MILLER

DEAN VILLAGE FROM ABOVE, LYDIA BOURHILL

DEAN VILLAGE FROM THE DEAN BRIDGE, CLIVE RAMAGE

DEAN VILLAGE, LIANA MORAN

ST BERNARD'S WELL, KATRINE LYCK

CIRCUS LANE, LAURA CAROLAN

CIRCUS LANE, ALAN GLASGOW

ST STEPHEN'S CHURCH, HUGH BRYDEN
LEFT: ST STEPHEN'S PLACE, STOCKBRIDGE, LINDSEY LAVENDER

DAZZLE ME LEITH, LIBBY WALKER

LEITH WALK, CASSANDRA HARRISON

LEITH, EILIDH MULDOON

LEITH TOWERBLOCK, KAREN WARNER

LEITH, ROB HAIN

THE SHORE, LEITH, DAVE THOMPSON

SOUTH LEITH PARISH CHURCH, SAM BLAIR

HAPPY DAYS AT PORTOBELLO, LYNN HANLEY

PORTOBELLO PROM, LINDSEY LAVENDER

AND THE SKIES SANG, LYNN HOWARTH

PORTOBELLO SUNRISE, LYNN HOWARTH

118

MORNINGSIDE TENEMENT, JOANNE FORBES

THE CANNY MAN'S PUB, LYDIA BOURHILL

A COSY CORNER OF THE CANNY MAN'S PUB, LYDIA BOURHILL

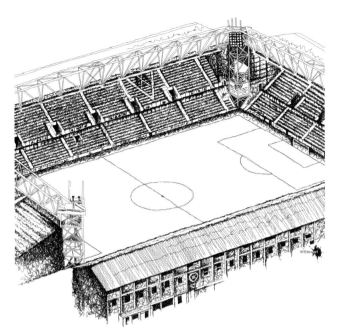

TYNECASTLE STADIUM, RACHEL STEWART

HIBS STADIUM, PAUL ISAACS

PLEWLANDS TERRACE, CAT OUTRAM

ARTISTS' CREDITS

Annie May Adam
Design and illustration combining
traditional printmaking and expressive
marks with digital collage
annie.may.adam@gmail.com
Pages 17, 66

Jane Askey
Landscape and still-life in a range
of media and techniques
www.janeaskey.com
Pages 13, 22, 71

Victoria Rose Ball
Detailed digital illustrations focusing
on architecture within Edinburgh and
hand lettered typography
www.victoriaroseball.com
Pages 55, 67, 81, 91

Alasdair Banks
International reputation for horse
racing paintings, his cityscapes reflect
the same spirited movement
www.alasdairbanks.com
Pages 13, 26, 80

Emma Bennett
Vibrant hand-cut collage using
recycled papers and hand-drawn
pictures
www.emmabennettcollage.co.uk
Page 30 and cover

Sam Blair
Maker of things. Illustrator at large
www.samblairillustrations.co.uk
Pages 36, 65, 115

Francis Boag
Joyous, expressionist interpretations
of the landscape of Scotland
www.francisboag.com
Page 22

Lydia Bourhill
Ink, watercolour and digital drawing
www.lydbourhill.wixsite.com/
bourhillustration
Pages 93, 104, 120

Richard Briggs
Pen and ink watercolour illustrations
of urban, coastal and rural landscapes
www.richardbriggs-illustration.co.uk
Pages 14–15, 38, 46, 98

Hugh Bryden
Printmaking artists books and
poetry pamphlets
www.hughbryden.com
Page 109

Laura Carolan
Mixed media drawing and illustration
exploring a sense of place
www.lauracarolan.co.uk
Pages 20, 106

Jonathan Chapman
Landscape and city illustrations
hand-painted with acrylic and ink
www.illustrationbyjonathan.com
Page 18–19

Liam Dobson
Oil on canvas, use of palette knife is a
vital of his artwork
www.Liamdobsonart.com
Pages 53, 102

Jenni Douglas
Hand pressed linocut
www.jennidouglas.co.uk
Pages 72, 83

Maria Doyle
Linocut prints, carved and
pulled by hand
www.instagram.com/maz.prints/
Pages 8–9, 41, 69

Yvette Earl
Hand-drawn and then digitally
coloured
www.yvette-earl.com
Page 37

Sally J Fisher
Collagraph prints hand-painted
with watercolour
www.sallyjfisher.com
Pages 28, 54

Joanne Forbes
Screen printing and drawings in a
range of media and subjects
joweegie@gmail.com
Pages 119

Alan Glasgow
Acrylic on canvas fine art paintings
alanglasgow5368@hotmail.co.uk
Pages 25, 107

Laura Gressani
Using printmaking to distill the
essential qualities of her subjects
www.lauragressani.com
Page 91

Rob Hain
A bird's-eye view of city life,
painted in acrylic on canvas
www.robhain.com
Pages 12, 21, 95, 97,114

Andrew Hamilton
Traditional fine ink drawings of
Scottish landmarks and architecture
www.ahamiltonsketches.com
Page 80–81

Lynn Hanley
Colourful, naïve style paintings
with quirky details and peppered
with tiny people
www.lynnhanley.com
Pages 23, 29,116

David Hardcastle
Continuous single line ink drawings
and places of cherished memories
chateau1000@gmail.com
Page 100–101

Cassandra Harrison
Maker of architectural artwork using
textiles, screen-printing, watercolour
and digital images
www.cassandraharrison.co.uk
Pages 82, 111

Sheenagh Harrison
Acrylic and mixed media cityscapes
and seascapes on canvas
www.sheenaghharrisonart.co.uk
Page 70

Claire Heminsley
The more you look the more you see!
www.incahoots.org.uk
Pages 27, 97

Rebecca Heselton
Artist, designer and illustrator
specialising in light pieces
www.rebeccaheselton.com
Page 103

Lynn Howarth
Pastel and acrylic paintings in a wide
range of subjects. Commissions
welcomed
www.lynnhowarth.co.uk
Page 118

Emily Ingrey-Counter
Drawings and paintings inspired by
the natural world
www.emilyingreycounter.com
Page 47

Paul Isaacs
Pen, ink and watercolour local
architectural studies
www.paulisaacs.co.uk
Pages 76, 121

Lucy Jones
Mixed media paintings and collage of
the Edinburgh Georgian architecture
www.lucyjonesart.com
Pages 90, 98

Hannah Kelly
Detailed pen and ink illustrations
of natural and urban landscapes
www.hannahkelly.co.uk
Page 74–75

Lindsey Lavender
Exploring rhythms of light and shade;
showing the everyday in a new light
www.lindseylavender.co.uk
Pages 60, 108, 117

Bob Lees
Former art teacher, creating
representational and semi-abstract
images. Acrylic and mixed-media
vallees@live.com
Pages 14, 57

Katrine Lyck
Danish illustration student at
Edinburgh College of Art focusing
on etchings
www.KatrineLyck.com
Page 106

Pam Mckenzie
Pam creates bright, vibrant expressive
paintings combining city views and
colourful wildflowers
Facebook: PamMckenzieArtist
Page 12

Hilke MacIntyre
Linocuts, woodcuts, ceramic
reliefs and paintings
www.macintyre-art.com
Page 48

Ross Macintyre
Watercolour and ink, paints
Edinburgh scenes, Scottish landscapes,
cityscapes, trees and flowers
www.rossmacintyre.com
Pages 15, 89, 94

Adrian B McMurchie
Known as The Glasgow
Illustrator, Adrian's architectural
watercolours have been a mainstay
in the Scottish commercial art scene
for over 20 years
www.amcmurchie.com
Pages 31, 34–35, 43, 61

Moy Mackay
Felted painting with dyed merino fibres and stitch
www.moymackaygallery.com
Pages 31, 42, 88

Sophie Martin
Artist and illustrator specialising in drawing from life in pen and watercolour
www.sophiemartinillustration.co.uk
Pages 40, 47, 48, 94

Ian Scott Massie
Portrays the personality of places through watercolour and screenprint
www.ianscottmassie.com
Pages 73, 96

Anna Middlemass
Digital paintings inspired by fairy-tales and wild places
www.annamiddlemass.com
Pages 77

Tomasz Mikutel
Watercolour artist born in Lodz (Poland), inspired by Joseph Zbukvic and Alvaro Castagnet
www.tomaszmikutel.com
Pages 64

Fiona Miller
Architectural illustrations in watercolour and ink-pen
www.fionamiller.net
Pages 33, 51

Kate Miller
Digital art and screen-prints
www.kate-miller.com
Pages 11, 23, 76, 104

Liana Moran
Large architectural drawings responding to the environment, structure and materials within cities
www.edinburghillustrations.com
Pages 44, 52, 105

Eilidh Muldoon
Hand-drawn linework and hand-printed textures arranged and coloured digitally
www.eilidhmuldoodles.com
Pages 59, 85, 112

Scott Naismith
Published Scottish semi-abstract painter. Scott uses expressive colour and exhibits worldwide
www.scottnaismith.com
Pages 100–101

Colm O'Brien
Colm O'Brien's articulate use of colour has attracted collectors world-wide
www.colmobrien.co.uk
Pages 24, 27, 32, 56, 102

Cat Outram
An etcher of cityscapes, landscape and all things that catch her eye
www.catoutramprintmaker.com
Pages 45, 122–123

Amanda Phillips
Amanda is a professional artist local to Edinburgh who exhibits all over Scotland
www.amandaphillips.co.uk
Pages 52

Clive Ramage
Atmospheric paintings and etchings of Scottish cities, land and seascapes
www.cliveramage.com
Pages 105

Lucy Roscoe
Illustration, artist's books and sculptural paper works. Illustrations commissioned for 'The Evergreen'
www.lucyroscoe.co.uk
Pages 67

Diana Savova
Realistic and fantasy paintings in different media including acrylic, watercolour and oil
www.artsavova.co.uk
Pages 58

Blythe Scott
Whimsical mixed media art, expressing an uplifting view of the world
www.blythescott.com
Pages 65, 84, 88, 89

Pamela Scott
Linocut prints
www.pamelascottprintmaker.com
Page 79

Sue Scullard
Black and white wood engravings
and pen drawings of landscape and
architecture
www.suescullard.co.uk
Pages 10, 78

Jenny Seddon
Handmade, limited-edition
screen-prints
www.jennyseddon.com
Map of Edinburgh

Esther Semmens
Detailed ink and watercolour
illustrations of architecture,
cityscapes and landscapes
www.estasketch.com
Pages 41, 84, 86–87, 99

Andrew Siddall
Architectural hand-drawn building
portraits and illustrations recording
city spaces and places
www.siddalldrawing.com
Page 62–63

Rachel Stewart
Rachel creates narrative
illustrations, digitally produced
in a scribble sketch style
www.rhstewart.com
Pages 44–45, 121

John Stoa
Dundee artist painting Scottish
landscapes, snow scenes, figures,
flowers and still life
www.johnstoa.com
Pages 20, 24, 49

Dave Thompson
Homage to iconic travel posters
rendered digitally in vector flat colour
www.davethompsonillustration.com
Pages 50, 115

Libby Walker
Libby's work celebrates the thriving
communities and sprawling
architecture of the city
www.libbywalker.co.uk
Pages 16, 68, 92, 110

Karen Warner
Energetic works created with oils,
pigment, beeswax, varnish and inks
www.karenwarner.co.uk
Pages 39, 113

Susie Wright
Screen-prints and drawings of
architecture, flora and fauna
www.susiewright.co.uk
Pages 32, 62–63

Every effort has been made to correctly credit contributors. In the case of any omissions or errors we would be pleased to make appropriate corrections in future editions.

ARTISTS